Contents

Off we go!

Beach

We set off in a ship.

We spot a beach.
It has cliffs and rocks.

Mangrove

This is a mangrove.
It has a lot of wet mud.

bat

mantis

moth

We spot a moth
and a bat!

Off we go!

Coral

This beach has sand.
The sun is hot.

coral

We spot fish
in the coral!

parrot fish

Off we go!

9

Ice

This beach has lots of ice!

We spot animals on the ice.
We spot fish as well.

cod

pup

Back we go!

Back We Go!

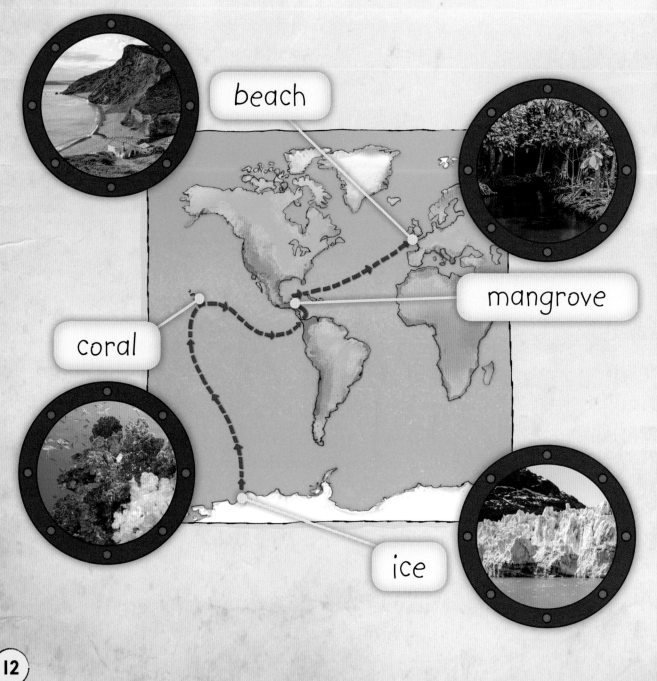

beach

mangrove

coral

ice